31 Vegetarian Brown Bag Lunches to Go

A Month of Easy Lunches for Busy People

Mary Scott

DISCLAIMER

Copyright © 2015 by Mary Scott.

All rights Reserved. No part of this publication or the information in it may be quoted from or reproduced in any form by means such as printing, scanning, photocopying or otherwise without prior written permission of the copyright holder.

Disclaimer and Terms of Use: Effort has been made to ensure that the information in this book is accurate and complete, however, the author and the publisher do not warrant the accuracy of the information, text and graphics contained within the book due to the rapidly changing nature of science, research, known and unknown facts and internet. The Author and the publisher do not hold any responsibility for errors, omissions or contrary interpretation of the subject matter herein. This book is presented solely for motivational and informational purposes only.

The recipes and information provided in this report are for educational purposes only and are not intended to provide dietary advice. Readers are strongly encouraged to consult a doctor before making the dietary changes that are required when switching to a Paleo food lifestyle. Recipe directions are provided as a guideline only as the quality of kitchen appliances varies and could result in the need for longer or shorter cooking times. All precautions should be taken to ensure food is fully cooked in order to prevent risk of foodborne illnesses. The author and publisher do not take responsibility for any consequences that are believed to be a result of following the instructions in this book.

Table of Contents

Introduction 1
Sandwiches and Wraps 2
   Veggie Hot Dog Wrap 2
   Mashed Avocado and Banana Sandwich 3
   Spinach and Black Bean Lettuce Wrap 4
   Speedy Burritos 6
   Vegetable Hoagies 7
   Tofu Lettuce Wraps 9
   Paneer Wrap 10
   Vegetarian Club Sandwich 11
   Mushroom Schezuan Wrap 12
   Tofu Salsa Lettuce Wrap 13
   Egg and Mushroom Wrap 15
Salads 16
   Mediterranean Salad 16
   Berry Spicy Salad 17
   Orange and Hazelnut Fennel Salad 18
   Creamy Mediterranean Platter 19
   Kale Crunch Salad 20
   Broccoli and Apple Salad 21
   Orange Extravaganza 22
   Spinach and Beet Salad 23
   Smoked Tofu Salad 24
Others 26

Squash and Parmesan Cakes...26

Microwaved Eggplant 27

Vegetarian Fajita Rice 28

Vegetarian Falafels..29

Broccoli Noodles 30

Pad Thai with Tofu 32

Cheesy Bruschetta 34

Zucchini Noodles 35

Fried Okra..36

Potato Pancakes to Go!...37

Spanish Rice 38

Conclusion..39

Introduction

Are you sick and tired of the same old PBJ lunch? When you are vegetarian, bringing a healthy lunch to work can be a real challenge! So, if you're looking for quick and easy, but healthy, lunch alternatives, look no further. This book is for you!

Included here, you will find 31 easy, delicious, and nutritious recipes to make your workday lunchtime easier and much less boring. Here you'll find eleven sandwiches and wraps, nine different salads, and eleven other delicious alternatives including delicious things like squash and parmesan cakes, fajita rice, falafels and more.

Each recipe in this collection includes:

1. Serving size,
2. Exact ingredients and measurements,
3. Step-by-step directions, and
4. Nutritional information.

I hope you enjoy making and eating these as much as my family does!

Mary

Sandwiches and Wraps

Veggie Hot Dog Wrap
Serves 2

Ingredients
2 sheets whole wheat lavash or other flat bread
2 vegetable hot dogs
1 cup chopped lettuce
⅓ cup grated carrots
2 tbsp tomato ketchup
2 tbsp. mustard

Directions
1. Cook vegetable hot dogs as per the instructions on the package.
2. Place hot dogs and chopped vegetables on lavash sheet.
3. Squeeze the tomato ketchup and mustard on top and wrap!

Nutritional Information
Calories: 280; Fats: 11g; Carbohydrates: 22g; Proteins: 13g

Mashed Avocado and Banana Sandwich
Serves 3

Ingredients
6 slices multigrain sandwich bread
1 avocado, coarsely mashed
2 ripe banana, sliced
3 tsp organic honey
1 tsp cardamom powder
2 tbsp. walnuts, finely chopped
1 tsp lemon juice
1 pinch salt

Directions
1. Except the bread slices, place all the remaining ingredients in a bowl and toss well.
2. Spoon out the ingredients on bread slices to make sandwiches.

Nutritional Information
Calories: 300; Fats: 16g; Carbohydrates: 19g; Proteins: 3g

Spinach and Black Bean Lettuce Wrap
Makes 4-6 wraps

Ingredients
2 cups baby spinach
2 cloves garlic (minced)
1 medium red onion (diced)
1 medium bell pepper (diced)
1 plantain (peeled and chopped)
1 can of black beans (drained and rinsed)
1 large chopped tomato
¼ cup vegetarian broth
½ tsp paprika
½ tbsp. chili Powder
1 tsp ground cumin
2 tbsp. olive oil
1 tbsp. lime juice
Sea salt to taste
1 ripe avocado (chopped)
4-6 Large Lettuce Leaves

Directions
1. Heat olive oil in a large skillet over medium heat. Sauté red onions and garlic until onions start to become soft and translucent.
2. Add bell pepper and plantain, sautéing until bell pepper has become softer.
3. Add baby spinach, black beans, broth, and tomatoes. Cook until spinach is just wilted.
4. Toss in all the spices, and lime juice, mixing well to making sure that the spices are all incorporated. Season with sea salt to taste.
5. Top with avocado before serving on lettuce wrap.

Nutritional Information

Calories: 442; Fats: 13g; Carbohydrates: 86g; Proteins: 59g

Speedy Burritos
Serves 2

Ingredients:
2 large wraps
2 tomatoes (deseeded, chopped)
4 eggs
3 spring onions (chopped)
1 red chili (sliced)
1 ¼ cup cheese (cheddar; grated)
1 cup milk
1 tsp vegetable oil
 Sour cream (to serve)

Directions:
1. In a mixing bowl, combine tomatoes with half of the red chili and half of the onions. Set aside.
2. In another bowl, whisk together the eggs with the milk. Set aside.
3. Heat oil in a large wok and fry the remaining onions and chili for approximately a minute or two. Add the egg mixture to the middle of the pan and allow it to cook for 3-4 minutes.
4. Remove from heat and add the cheese. Mix well.
5. Spoon the mix into the wraps and put it in your lunch box along with the home made salsa (step 1) and sour cream.

Nutritional Information
Calories: 611; Fats: 38g; Carbohydrates: 33g; Proteins: 35g

Vegetable Hoagies
Serves 4

Ingredients:
1 can artichoke hearts
¼ cup red onion (sliced into rings)
1 tomato (sliced)
1 tbsp. olive oil
2 tbsp. balsamic vinegar
1 tsp. oregano
2 slices cheese (provolone)
1 baguette
¼ cup pepperoncini (sliced)
2 cup romaine lettuce (shredded)

Directions:
1. Place the onion rings in a bowl. Cover with water. Set this bowl aside.
2. In another bowl, combine the oregano, oil, vinegar, tomato, and artichoke hearts.
3. Cut the baguette into 4 pieces. Split the pieces horizontally and take out about half the bread from both sides.
4. Drain the onions and make sure they are dry before continuing.
5. Assemble the sandwiches. Take the provolone and divide it between the four pieces of baguette bread on the bottom.
6. Spread the artichoke mixture over the bread on both sides.
7. Top the sandwich with the pepperoncini, lettuce, and onion. Cover with the tops of the baguette and serve.

Nutritional Information
Calories: 264; Fats: 8g; Carbohydrates: 39g; Proteins: 14g

Tofu Lettuce Wraps
Serves 16

Ingredients
Filling
1 lb. tofu (extra-firm, crumbled)
1 onion (chopped)
1 tbsp. ginger (minced)
2 cloves garlic (minced)
4 tbsp. soy sauce
4 tbsp. hoisin sauce
8 oz water chestnuts (chopped)
2 tsp olive oil
2 tsp vegetarian chili sauce
16 iceberg lettuce leaves

Topping
1 carrot (peeled and grated)
½ cup green onions (chopped)
½ cup cashews (chopped)
Hoisin and chili sauces (to taste)

Directions:
1. Heat oil in a large skillet on medium heat.
2. Add onion, ginger, and garlic, cooking for about 7 to 10 minutes or until onions are translucent and start turning brown.
3. Add tofu (crumbling it before adding) and water chestnuts; cook for 4 minutes, or until just heated through. Stir in the hoisin sauce, soy sauce, and chili sauce.
4. Spoon on top of the lettuce leaves and roll up.

Nutritional Information
Calories: 93; Fats: 4.5g; Carbohydrates: 10.2g; Proteins: 4.4g

Paneer Wrap
Serves 1

Ingredients
6 ounces Paneer (cubed)
2 garlic cloves (peeled, chopped)
1 bell pepper (green, chopped)
1 onion (chopped)
2 tbsp Thai sweet chili sauce
½ tsp Sea salt
½ tsp black pepper
1 tsp olive oil
2 iceberg lettuce leaves

Directions
1. Fry the paneer on high heat in a hot skillet with oil, constantly tossing so that it browns on all sides and doesn't burn.
2. Add garlic, bell pepper and onions, stirring well and sautéing for 2 minutes before adding the sweet chili sauce and seasonings.
3. Serve on lettuce leaves.

Nutritional Information
Calories: 252; Fats: 8g; Carbohydrates: 21.4g; Proteins: 22.8g

Vegetarian Club Sandwich
Serves 1

Ingredients

3 slices multi grain bread (toasted)
1 large handful of baby spinach
2 tomatoes, thickly sliced
1 carrot, peeled and coarsely grated
2 tsp reduced-fat hummus /or mashed (very ripe) avocado
Juice of half a lemon
1 tbsp. olive oil

Directions

1. Mix carrot, baby spinach, lemon juice, and olive oil together.
2. Spread hummus over each slice of toast.
3. Top a slice of toast with the baby spinach salad, layering with another slice of toast and then top with the tomato. Put the final slice of toast with hummus side down on top and, then press down cutting the sandwich into two before eating.

Nutritional Information:
Calories 189; Total Fat 14.6g; Total Carbohydrates 15.4g; Protein 2.8g

Mushroom Schezuan Wrap

Serves 4

Ingredients

1 ½ tsp ginger-garlic paste
½ cup spring onion whites (chopped finely)
½ cup carrots (julienned)
4 tsp schezuan sauce
3 cups mushrooms (sliced)
1 tbsp oil
 Sea salt to taste
4 lettuce leaves

Directions

1. Heat pan with oil. Add the ginger-garlic paste and spring onions. Sauté on medium heat, until they turn translucent.
2. Add carrots and the schezuan sauce, sautéing on medium heat for another 2 to 3 minutes.
3. Add mushrooms and sea salt, mixing gently and cook for another minute, while stirring continuously.
4. Arrange wraps by spooning mixing onto lettuce leaves.

Nutritional Information

Calories: 47; Fats: 3.7g; Carbohydrates: 3g; Proteins: 1.8g

Tofu Salsa Lettuce Wrap
Serves 8

Ingredients
½ lb tofu (extra firm, sliced)
1 onion (red, sliced)
1 Mexican squash or zucchini (sliced)
½ bell pepper (green, sliced)
½ bell pepper (red, sliced)
1 cup button mushrooms (sliced)
1 cup black beans (boiled, drained)
2 cups baby spinach (chopped)
1 tbsp taco seasoning
2 tbsp salsa
1 tbsp olive oil
Sea salt to taste
1 head iceberg lettuce

Directions:
1. Sprinkle taco seasoning over the tofu and leave it for 10 minutes.
2. Grill tofu on both sides on a hot griddle that has been sprayed with cooking spray. Cut the tofu into bite sized pieces.
3. Heat a wok with oil and add onion sautéing for 2 minutes, or until it becomes translucent. Add squash, mushrooms, bell peppers, and spinach. Add sea salt to taste.
4. Sauté for another 3-4 minutes on high heat and add the grilled tofu strips, salsa black beans, and any taco seasoning that is remaining, mixing well.
5. Serve on lettuce leaves.

Nutritional Information
Calories: 120; Fats: 2.2g; Carbohydrates: 19.5g; Proteins: 6.4g

Egg and Mushroom Wrap
Serves 1

Ingredients
2 large eggs
1 cup mushrooms (any, chopped)
1 green chili (thinly sliced)
Salt and pepper to taste
1 pinch paprika
Coconut oil to cook
Parmesan cheese to garnish
Lettuce leaves

Directions
1. Whisk the eggs in a bowl with green chili, salt, pepper and paprika. Heat oil in a frying pan and pour in the eggs.
2. Sprinkle mushrooms over it and scramble the eggs slightly with a spatula.
3. Sprinkle cheese before wrapping in lettuce leaves.

Nutritional Information
Calories: 159; Fats: 10.1g; Carbohydrates: 3.3g; Proteins: 14.8g

Salads

Mediterranean Salad
Makes 4 servings

Ingredients
2 cups tomatoes (Sliced)
1 cup cucumber (peeled, chopped)
⅓ cup yellow bell pepper (diced)
¼cup radishes (sliced)
¼ cup flat-leaf parsley (chopped)
1 clove of garlic (minced)
1 tbsp lemon juice
3 tbsp extra-virgin olive oil
2 cups baby spinach (torn up)
Black pepper and sea salt (to taste)

Directions
1. In a large salad bowl, mix together bell pepper, cucumber, radishes, tomatoes, and parsley.
2. Sprinkle lemon juice, oil, and garlic on the salad. Mix well. Add salt and pepper to taste. Lay salad over the baby spinach and serve.

Nutritional Information:
Calories 198; Fat 7g; Carbohydrates 11.5g;
Protein 22g

Berry Spicy Salad

Makes 2 servings

Ingredients
1 jalapeño pepper
4 tbsp lime juice
¼ tsp cumin (ground)
4 tbsp olive oil
4 cups baby greens (mixed)
2 cups fresh blackberries or raspberries (or try 1 cup of each!)
¼ cup red onion (sliced thinly)

Directions
1. Remove seeds from jalapeño and mince the pepper flesh.
2. Put olive oil, lime juice, cumin, and 2 tsp of minced jalapeño in a blender. Blend until smooth.
3. Toss dressing over greens, berries, and onion. Serve.

Nutritional Information:
Calories 403; Fat 28.9g; Carbohydrates 37.1g; Protein 8.7g

Orange and Hazelnut Fennel Salad
Makes 6 servings

Ingredients
3 bulbs fennel
6 navel oranges
⅓ cup orange juice (fresh is best)
1 tsp hazelnuts (chopped finely)
1 tbsp fresh orange zest
2 tbsp extra-virgin olive oil

Directions
1. Slice fennel bulbs finely. Peel oranges and carefully slice away the white membrane.
2. Arrange oranges on top of fennel. Sprinkle with hazelnuts. Sprinkle with oil and orange juice. Add a touch of zest to finish it off.

Nutritional Information:
Calories 233; Fat 12.9; Carbohydrates 27.1g; Protein 11g

Creamy Mediterranean Platter
Serves 2

Ingredients:
1 cup chopped English cucumber
1 cup sundried chopped tomatoes
⅓ cup chopped yellow bell pepper
½ cup juicy carrots, chopped
½ cup tender beets, chopped
¾ cup chopped lettuce

Dressing
½ cup chopped parsley
6 tbsp low fat mayonnaise
1 tsp white pepper
½ tsp Italian seasoning
Salt for taste

Directions
1. Mix dressing ingredients in a bowl. Add all remaining ingredients.
2. Toss well and serve.

Nutritional Information

Calories: 205; Fats: 15g; Carbohydrates: 28g; Proteins: 2g

Kale Crunch Salad
Makes 1-2 servings

Ingredients
1 bunch of kale (medium-size)
1 carrot (shredded)
½ cup golden beets (finely cut)
Lemon juice (use 1.5 lemons)
Lemon zest (use 1 lemon)
1 tbsp olive oil
Sea salt and black pepper to taste
¼ cup of your favorite chopped nuts (walnuts, almonds, pecans, etc.)

Directions
1. Cut kale leaves thinly and place into a large bowl.
2. Add carrots, beets, lemon juice, lemon zest, olive oil, salt, and pepper. Stir well.
3. Allow salad to sit for 10-20 minutes so that the vegetables can soften a bit.
4. Top with the chopped nuts of your choice.

Nutritional Information:
Calories 276; Fat 8g; Carbohydrates 17g; Protein 13.4g

Broccoli and Apple Salad
Serves 4

Ingredients:
Salad:
2 heads of broccoli (chopped)
1 large grated carrot
½ cup walnuts (chopped)
¼ cup cranberries (dried)
1 medium size apple (cored and chopped)
¼ cup onion (chopped)

Dressing:
1 cup mayonnaise
1 tsp honey (raw)
2 ½ tbsp lemon juice
1 garlic clove (minced)
¼ tsp sea salt
Black pepper (to taste)

Directions:
1. Combine the dressing ingredients in a medium sized bowl. Mix well and season to taste.
2. In another bowl, add broccoli, carrot, cranberries, apple, walnut and onion.
3. Pour dressing over the salad and mix well.
4. Serve warm or cold.

Nutritional Information:
Calories 338; Fat 29.2g; Carbohydrates 38.9g; Protein 6g

Orange Extravaganza
Makes 4 servings

Ingredients
2 carrots (shredded)
3 cups romaine lettuce (chopped)
1 navel orange (each slice cut in half)
2 cups papaya (dried)
2 tbsp fresh ginger (shredded)
Lime juice (use 1 lime)
1-2 tbsp. honey (to taste)
1 tbsp olive oil
Dash black pepper
Dash sea salt

Directions
1. Mix orange, carrots, lettuce, and papaya in a big salad bowl and set aside.
2. Combine ginger, honey, lime juice, olive oil, pepper, and salt. Stir well. Toss dressing with salad and serve.

Nutritional Information:
Calories 122; Fat 6g; Carbohydrates 12.5g; Protein 8g

Spinach and Beet Salad

Serves: 4, 2 cups each

Ingredients:
8 cups of baby spinach
1 tbsp. of olive oil
1 cup of red onion, chopped
2 tomatoes, chopped
2 tbsp. of Kalamata olives, sliced
2 tbsp. of parsley
1 clove of garlic, minced
2 cups of beets, thinly sliced
2 tbsp. of balsamic vinegar
¼ tsp of salt
¼ tsp of pepper

Directions:

1. Put spinach in the bowl.
2. Heat oil in the skillet on medium heat.
3. Cook red onion for 2 minutes.
4. Add chopped tomatoes and olives.
5. Add garlic and parsley, cook for 3 minutes.
6. Add sliced beets to skillet with salt and pepper and vinegar; cook for one more minute.
7. Add beet mixture to spinach and mix well.
8. Serve and enjoy.

Nutritional Values:

Calories: 122 kcal Fats: 5 grams Carbohydrates: 17 grams Protein: 4 grams

Smoked Tofu Salad
Serves: 6

Ingredients:
2 cups water
¾ tsp salt
1 cup quinoa
¼ cup lemon juice
3 tbsp. olive oil
2 cloves garlic, minced
¼ tsp pepper
8 ounces smoked tofu, diced
1 yellow bell pepper, diced
1 cup grape tomatoes, halved
1 cup diced cucumber
½ cup mint
½ cup parsley
Dash salt

Directions:
1. Bring water and ¾ tsp salt to boil in a saucepan.
2. Add quinoa and reduce to a simmer, cook for 20 minutes.
3. Remove from heat and spread equally onto the baking sheet, let cool for 10 minutes.
4. Mix lemon juice, oil, dash of salt and pepper together in the bowl.
5. Mince garlic and add to bowl.
6. Add diced bell pepper, cucumber and tomato into bowl along with the mint and the parsley.
7. Add tofu and combine well.
8. Serve and enjoy.

Nutritional Information:

Calories: 228 kcal Fats: 10 grams Carbohydrates: 26 grams Protein: 9 grams

Others

Squash and Parmesan Cakes
Serves: 4

Ingredients:
1 egg
2/3 cup shallots, chopped
1 tbsp. parsley
¼ tsp salt
¼ tsp pepper
2 cups summer squash, shredded
½ cup parmesan cheese
1 tbsp. olive oil

Directions:

1. Preheat oven to 400 degrees.
2. Beat egg in mixing bowl.
3. Add salt, pepper, and parsley.
4. Cut and add shallots.
5. Add cheese and squash.
6. Heat oil in skillet on medium heat.
7. Divide the mixture into 4 sections.
8. Flatten each section out on the skillet.
9. Cook each side for 3 minutes.
10. Put the cakes onto the pan and place in the oven.
11. Bake for 10 minutes.
12. Remove from heat.
13. Serve and enjoy.

Nutritional Information:

Calories: 130 kcal Fats: 8 grams Carbohydrates: 9 grams Protein: 7 grams

Microwaved Eggplant

Serves: 1

Ingredients:
1 eggplant
½ tsp salt
½ tsp pepper
1 tbsp. olive oil
1 tbsp. lemon juice

Directions:

1. Dice eggplant and place in a microwavable mug or a mason jar.
2. Cover with olive oil, lemon juice and seasonings. Mix well.
3. Place in microwave and cook for 7 minutes. Use extreme caution when removing from the microwave! The glass will be very hot.
4. Allow it to cool before serving.

Nutritional Information:

Calories: 241   Fats: 15.0 g Carbohydrates: 27.9 g Protein: 4.7 g

Vegetarian Fajita Rice

Serves 4

Ingredients:
1 cup Brown rice (cooked)
14 oz black eyed beans (canned, drained)
1 jar roasted peppers in olive oil
1 lime (juiced)
3 tbsp. fresh coriander (roughly chopped)
2 tbsp. fajita seasoning mix
1 tbsp. olive oil

Directions:
1. In a large skillet, heat one tbsp. olive oil on low heat.
2. Add peppers and fajita seasoning and cook for approximately a minute or two.
3. Stir in rice and beans and cook for an additional 4-6 minutes.
4. Add remaining oil from peppers along with lime juice and chopped coriander.
5. Cook for approximately two to three minutes and serve!
6. Pack in airtight plastic container. Heat in microwave before serving!

Nutritional Information:

Calories: 303   Fats: 11.0 g Carbohydrates: 46 g
Protein: 8 g

Vegetarian Falafels
Serves 6

Ingredients:
1 can chickpeas (drained)
1 egg (beaten)
1 onion (chopped finely)
1 garlic clove (crushed)
1 tsp coriander
1 tsp cumin powder
2 tbsp. + ½ cup sunflower oil
1 tsp parsley (chopped)

Directions:
1. Heat 2 tbsp. sunflower oil in a large skillet over low heat. Add onion and garlic and sauté for approximately 5-7 minutes.
2. Add the drained chickpeas, cumin powder and coriander to the skillet and mash the chickpeas while cooking on low heat.
3. Stir in the parsley followed by the beaten egg and cook for another 3-4 minutes.
4. Pour the mixture into the bowl and mould it into six equal sized patties.
5. Heat the remaining oil and fry the patties over medium high heat for approximately 2 minutes on each side or until they turn golden.
6. Pack the falafels in airtight plastic container along with your favorite veggies.

Nutritional Information:

Calories: 105; Fats: 6g; Carbohydrates: 8g; Proteins: 5g

Broccoli Noodles
Serves 2

Ingredients:
2 nests egg noodles
8 ounces chestnut mushrooms (sliced)
1 head broccoli (cut into florets)
1 can vegetable stock
4 spring onions (sliced)
1 garlic clove (chopped)
2 tbsp sesame oil
½ tsp chili flakes
2 tbsp hoisin sauce
2 tbsp cashew nuts
2 cups water

Directions:
1. Pour two cups of water into a pan. Add vegetable stock to it and bring it to boil.
2. Add egg noodles and cook for approximately 3-4 minutes.
3. Add broccoli florets and cook for an additional two minutes.
4. Reserve approximately a cup of the stock and drain remaining liquid from noodles.
5. In a large skillet, add sesame oil and stir fry mushrooms until they turn golden. Add chili flakes along with onions, and garlic and cook for approximately a minute or two.
6. Add noodles and broccoli to skillet along with the hoisin sauce and 3-4 tbsp. of the stock. Mix well.
7. Spoon the noodles into airtight plastic container, using a pair of tongs and garnish with nuts and onion.

Nutritional Information:

Calories: 624; Fats: 14g; Carbohydrates: 105g; Proteins: 25g

Pad Thai with Tofu
Serves 4

Ingredients

2 eggs (whisked together lightly)
1 tbsp. tamarind paste
2 tbsp. (light) sweet chili sauce
3 garlic cloves (chopped)
10 ½ ounces firm tofu (cut into cubes)
1 nest egg noodles
6 spring onions (thinly sliced)
1 ½ cups bean sprouts
Handful coriander leaves and salted peanuts
Juice of 1 lime
1 lime cut into wedges
2 tbsp. olive oil
Sea salt to taste

Directions

1. Cook noodles according to the packet instructions.
2. Mix tamarind sauce, lime juice, and sweet chili sauce in a small bowl.
3. Heat 1 tbsp. oil in a non-stick wok and fry the tofu for about 8 minutes, until golden on all sides. Set aside in a bowl.
4. Scramble eggs in 1 tbsp. oil. Set aside in the bowl with tofu.
5. Stir-fry spring onions, bean sprouts, and garlic cooking for 2 minutes. Toss in drained egg

noodles, the sauce you mixed and some sea salt.
6. Stir in tofu and eggs; heat through. Serve with some chopped coriander, salted peanuts, and lime wedges.

Nutritional Information:
Calories 210; Total Fat 7.2g; Total Carbohydrates 23.9g; Protein 15.0g

Cheesy Bruschetta

Serves 8

Ingredients:
1 jar artichoke hearts (marinated, chopped and drained)
⅓ cup onions (red, sliced)
5 tbsp mayonnaise
½ cup Romano cheese (grated)
1 French baguette (thickly sliced)

Directions:

1. Preheat broiler.
2. In a mixing bowl, combine marinated artichoke hearts with sliced onions, cheese and mayonnaise.
3. Spoon on top of the baguette slices and arrange the slices on a large baking sheet.
4. Broil the slices in the preheated oven for approximately 2-3 minutes or until the topping turns light brown.
5. Pack in airtight plastic container and enjoy!

Nutritional Information:

Calories: 278; Fats: 11.1g; Carbohydrates: 35.7g; Proteins: 10g

Zucchini Noodles
Serves 6

Ingredients:
12 ounces egg noodles (cooked)
3 tbsp olive oil
4 ounces cream cheese
4 cups zucchini (shredded)
½ cup low fat milk
½ cup basil (chopped, fresh)
2 garlic cloves (minced)
Salt (to taste)
Pepper (to taste)
Grated Parmesan Cheese (for garnishing)

Directions:

1. In a large skillet, heat three tbsp. of olive oil over medium high heat.
2. Stir in garlic and cook for approximately 2-3 minutes. Add the shredded zucchini and cook for an additional 10-12 minutes.
3. Add half cup of low fat milk to skillet along with the cream cheese and basil. Mix well.
4. Season with salt and pepper and cook for an additional minute or two.
5. Transfer into airtight plastic container and garnish the noodles with grated Parmesan cheese.

Nutritional Information:

Calories: 379; Fats: 17.4g; Carbohydrates: 44.1g; Proteins: 12.4g

Fried Okra

Serves 4

Ingredients:
10 okra pods (sliced)
1 cup corn meal
1 egg (beaten)
½ cup vegetable oil
¼ tsp salt
¼ tsp black pepper

Directions:

1. Place egg mix in a small bowl and soak sliced okra in it.
2. In another bowl, mix together corn meal, salt and pepper.
3. Heat oil in a large wok over medium high heat.
4. Dredge sliced okra pods in the cornmeal mix and cook in hot oil until they turn golden.
5. Serve with your favorite dip.

Nutritional Information:

Calories: 394; Fats: 29.2g; Carbohydrates: 29g; Proteins: 4.7g

Potato Pancakes to Go!
Serves 10

Ingredients
2 cups potatoes (peeled, boiled and mashed)
¼ cup Cheddar cheese (shredded)
1 egg (beaten)
1 tbsp butter
1 tsp salt

Directions:
1. In a large mixing bowl, whisk together egg with mashed potatoes, cheese and salt.
2. Heat butter in a griddle over medium high heat.
3. Spoon the mixture onto the butter laden griddle; approximately ¼ cup at a time and flatten it.
4. Fry the potato pancakes until they turn golden on each side.
5. Place in airtight plastic container along with your favorite veggies and/or dip.

Nutritional Information:

Calories: 254; Fats: 14.5g; Carbohydrates: 23.9g; Proteins: 7.2g

Spanish Rice
Serves 4

Ingredients:
1 cup white rice (uncooked)
1 small jar of salsa
2 cups water
1 tsp garlic (minced)

Directions:
1. Place uncooked rice with minced garlic in a large sauce pan.
2. Top it off with water and salsa. Bring to boil.
3. Allow the rice to simmer for approximately 20-25 minutes.
4. Pack in airtight plastic container and enjoy!

Nutritional Information:

Calories: 200; Fats: 0.5g; Carbohydrates: 44.2g; Proteins: 5.1g

Conclusion

People who embrace the vegetarian lifestyle are generally health conscious. I hope you have enjoyed this collection of healthy lunch ideas to add variety to what is otherwise often boring choices.

As we all know, taking your lunch with you every day is usually much healthier and less expensive than eating out. Often, it is hard to find places that serve quick, yet healthy and inexpensive lunch alternatives. Most often, it is easier and more affordable to just pack your lunch and bring it with you when you go to work.

Wouldn't you rather grab something delicious, more nutritious, and less expensive and enjoy it than spend your time waiting for more expensive, less healthy and often bland food?

I know I would!

Mary

Made in the USA
Lexington, KY
10 March 2019